Imagine an equilateral triangle
bearing the burden of sameness
knowing that that was possible only
in geometry —

mpT
MODERN POETRY
IN TRANSLATION
The best of world poetry

No. 1 2024

ISSN (print) 0969-3572
ISSN (online) 2052-3017
ISBN (print) 978-1-910485-38-5

Managing Editor: Sarah Hesketh
Digital Content Editor: Ed Cottrell
Finance Manager: Deborah de Kock
Creative Apprentice: Chloe Elliott

Design by Brett Evans Biedscheid
Cover Art by Liliana Dmitrovic
Typesetting by Libanus Press Ltd
Proofreader: Katy Evans-Bush

Printed and bound in Great Britain by Charlesworth Press, Wakefield
For submissions and subscriptions please visit
www.modernpoetryintranslation.com

Modern Poetry in Translation Limited. A Company Limited by Guarantee
Registered in England and Wales, Number 5881603 UK
Registered Charity Number 1118223

LOTTERY FUNDED
Supported using public funding by
ARTS COUNCIL
ENGLAND

Cover description: A series of embroidered lyrics cover a white linen bed sheet. The words appear in lowercase script. The first lyric in blue thread appears on the left and reads "a song of / how did we / get / here". The second lyric in red thread appears lower down, on the right, and reads "a song of / never quite / belong / (not knowing / how to). The final lyric appears at the bottom, in blue thread, and reads "a song of / bombing / the hell / out of my / childhood." The three verses overlap, sharing occasional lines, flowing from one piece of the text to the next.

Above: On the left, the Arts Council England logo curves around in a circle, next to a black outline of a hand crossing fingers. Underneath both images, 'LOTTERY FUNDED' is written. In a line on the right, the text reads, 'Supported using public funding by ARTS COUNCIL ENGLAND'.

MODERN POETRY IN TRANSLATION

Bearing the Burden of Sameness: Focus on Care

CONTENTS

Focus

Reviews

EDITORIAL

By Sarah Hesketh, Managing Editor

There's a quote I come back to often: 'Quite, quite', thought Too-ticky with a little sigh. 'It's always like this in their adventures. To save and be saved. I wish somebody would write a story sometime about the people who warm up the heroes afterwards'. It appears in Finnish writer Tove Jansson's masterpiece, *Moominland Midwinter.* Characterised as wise, practical and compassionate, Too-ticky was based on Jansson's long-term life partner, the Finnish graphic artist Tuulikki 'Tooti' Pietilä, a woman whom Jansson credited with being a calm and sustaining presence that enabled Jansson's creativity, and supported her through depression and the pressures of her Moomin-induced fame.

To inhabit the role of carer is to take on a back-stage role in someone else's story. Someone else's needs – for medication, for food, for a more comfortable position to sit in or lie down; taken on willingly – or not (and sometimes an intense mixture of both), the needs of others become more pressing to you than your own desires or priorities in life (I'll leave the translators amongst you to draw your own parallels). This issue of *MPT*, with a focus on care, features a brilliant range of poetry that hopes to tell some stories of 'those who warm up the heroes afterwards'. It is, necessarily, a poetry that foregrounds need, as can be seen in the raw expression of Ilmar Lehtpere's 'We are walking together' where the poet's partner turns to him and, after a long struggle, finally finds the ability to simply say '*Please always come and help me*'. It is a poetry where the body is forever making itself more present. Beth Hickling-Moore's translation of Carla Nyman's sinuous poems concludes: 'who am i | a succession of unlovings | tangled with the gastric body'. In Vivan Lamarque's work, translated by Vilma De Gasperin and N.S. Thompson from Italian 'the gold | of the urine sack shines'.

Systems of care are both life-saving and oppressive. Brynjulf Jung Tjønn's work, translated by Rachel Rankin, explores the after-effects of being adopted from a Korean children's home into a rural Norwegian community. Abdullah O. Jimoh's poem 'My Brother' reminds us that families can be found. Both Ranajit Das' poem 'Sharmila's Loneliness', translated by Bidisha Mukherjee, and Xinyang Wu's 'The River Snail Maiden', translated by Tuoya Wulan, emphasise that care is a feminist issue. The burden of care, both historically and today, falls disproportionately on women.

'What good's a good intention for recycling?' asks Ailbhe Ní Ghearbhuigh in translation by Billy Ramsell. Our duty of care to the planet, how we are failing in it, and what we might learn from ecological systems of support, also runs through this issue. Despite the often overwhelming anxieties and pressures of contemporary life, the speaker in Adriana Lisboa's poem, translated by Alison Entrekin, urges themself to remember that:

> none of this exempts me
> from the flood of the moment
> from taking to the streets against the intolerable
> from clearing the weeds that threaten the gerberas
> from waiting a few seconds

Opposite: In black and white, various photographs of various former MPT contributors in three rows of six. Below are the MPT logo and motto, 'The best of world poetry', and a quote from John Berger, saying 'ANYONE WHO WANTS TO CHANGE THE WORLD AND SEE IT CHANGED SHOULD JOIN MPT'. Below that is the ACE logo, as well as a line describing MPT, our social media information, website, and subscription info (£29 a year – UK Subscription, £44 – International Subscription).

Those few seconds are given over to a small moment of care in pouring coffee for a friend. Small gestures enable us to continue, even though, as Cătălina Florina Florescu writes in her self-translation, '… life is strife | and light | and poorly cut out shapes', but 'you | of all people, you | are awake: | Imagine that'.

At the time of writing, there is still no ceasefire in Gaza. And so we start this issue with new translations by Kareem James Abu-Zeid of three poems by contemporary Palestinian poet Najwan Darwish. In his poem 'Spring' Darwish writes: 'Spring was running late, so late | that my nightmare became | the spring itself'. The nightmare is real and ongoing for millions of people right now. Also extremely important, is the sentiment expressed here by Dutch poet Ester Naomi Perquin, translated in this issue by David Colmer, that poetry is 'not bread, not oxygen cylinders, not education'. We have paid all our contributors as usual for this issue, but we have asked, where they might be able, if they might consider donating a portion of their fee to a charity which provides direct aid to Gaza.

Perquin ends the same poem suggesting that poetry can speak to 'every fish that's not yet lost'. *MPT* has always strived to help the voices of those in conflict zones to travel and be heard more widely by a global community in solidarity. Rohingya poetry, work by Uyghur writers and many more communities who continue to suffer extreme violence and oppression will always have a home in *MPT*, often long after the news cycle has changed and the cameras have departed. We would urge you to seek out these voices in our archive, to keep on reading and listening to them.

It has been an absolute privilege and a pleasure to step out of my own usual back-stage role as Managing Editor, to caretaker-edit this issue of *MPT* whilst the recruitment process for our new Editor was completed. We look forward very much to welcoming them to the team and the wider *MPT* community shortly. My huge thanks to all of our contributors to this issue for their patience and wonderful work. Artist and carer Liliana Dmitrovic has allowed us to feature images of her beautiful embroidery as the cover art for this issue, for which we're very grateful. Also many thanks to our outgoing Editor Khairani Barokka for her brilliant commissioning and selection of much of the material in the front section of this issue. To the *MPT* Board, who are also a back-stage presence who give so much of their time and expertise to *MPT* for free, thank you. And to the team – Ed, Chloe and Debbie, who sustain and warm me up continually. Sameness can be a burden. It can also be a vital joy.

About the cover: Our cover image for this issue is by Liliana Dmitrovic. Liliana's current work explores ideas of remembering, belonging and not belonging, the language of symbols and principles we embrace or reject. The piece 'Songs of the three colours' is part of this exploration, of looking for clues of how we are. Liliana grew up with women who did sewing and knitting and crochet. Embroidering the songs created the direct connection to those other times. There are now 14 songs of the three colours and they can be read or sung in any order. To find out more about her work, visit https://eljaydeeart.wordpress.com

NAJWAN DARWISH

Translated by Kareem James Abu-Zeid from Arabic

I am very pleased to present in English translation three poems by Najwan Darwish, one of the most prominent Arab poets writing today. His work is inextricably bound up with his homeland of Palestine, the endless Occupation, and the countless horrors that have been imposed on its population, including those of the present moment. His relationship with the land and its history is a complex one, as we can see here, for it is a place of loss as much as anything else, and it is only 'doubtfully' that one can even call it a country.

When Spring Comes

I told you I saw the land being led to the slaughter.
These are nightmares, you said,
they'll end when spring comes
to the door of your home.

Spring was running late, so late
that my nightmare became
the spring itself.
I can't bring the land
down from on high,
and I don't know who hung her there,
and all I can find is my own self
to take my vengeance on:
'You were the one
who hung her.... You were the one'.

Convinced it hung the land, my self
refuses to wake
from the throes of remorse.

Comparisons

'Days more bitter than the Road to Golgotha' –
a comparison
that no longer holds.

'Days more bitter than the Path of Thorns' –
this one's from the mind of a shepherd
who never tended any sheep
(if she really *were* a shepherd, she'd know
that thorns are part and parcel of the pasture).

'Days of sweetness soon turned cold and bitter' –
this may have come from a person
who'd realized something once, but promptly
let all their knowledge slip away.

My Lost Letter

Give it back to me,
the wall of despair that propped me up,
the one I wrote behind,
in whose shadows my words turned to truth.
Give me back the pagan summer,
the infidel winter,
and life on the edge,
and the fall from it.
Then, by some miracle, one's life isn't lost,
instead it continues
stoking anxiety
in the trenches of ancient empires
that historians have come to pity.

Bring back the loss that's regal, gilded,
for without it the exile can no longer be king.
And bring her down, for a little while, from the cross
so she can rest –
that one hanging between Galilee and Jerusalem,
the one we doubtfully call a country.
I wrote her a letter in my youth, a letter
that kept getting lost, that never arrived,
and I've been at it for years now,
trying to find it,
until I myself became
my lost letter.

ALYA KHAITLINA

Translated by Alexandra Berlina from Russian

Alya, who is married to a Ukrainian and was pregnant when the invasion started, became a tireless volunteer for the refugees. Somehow, while coordinating routes and finding homes for families fleeing the war, she also managed to react to the news with a series of poems that continues to this day. Some of these poems stuck in my head so badly that I simply had to translate them; another translation will be published in the *Massachusetts Review* later this year.

War Poem 276

Flowers, exhausted. The autumn sun, hardly shining.
Howl in your throat? Reciting some verse will do.
Gossamer thin, the life lines on palms so tiny.
It's such an easy business to cut them through.
The pillow is hardly creased by the baby's weight.
Under the hoarfrost, his lashes seem even longer.
He had been born so small. Cold, so cold. Too late.
Just for a short few days, life was allowed to linger.
He seems alive, all that's missing is breathing,
as if he was sleeping happily through the din.
Everyone's crying. She is crying and freezing:
Her sweater is soaked right through. The milk has come in.

ESTER NAOMI PERQUIN

Four Poems from *Unsolicited Advice* (2022)
translated by David Colmer from Dutch

Whether poetry or prose, Ester Naomi Perquin's work is characterised by the sharp-eyed humanity of its perspective and the precision of the writing. While Perquin returns frequently to the domestic and familial, her themes range wider and encompass society as a whole, literature and, as shown in this short selection, politics and international relations. Her most frequently cited biographical fact is the way she put herself through writing school by working as a prison guard, and this illustrates both her dedication to craft and her willingness to engage with people who are seldom represented in contemporary Dutch-language poetry, not just prisoners but also guards. The result was the prize-winning *Cell Inspections* (2012), a largely thematic collection that is one of the highlights of her work so far (and would make a fascinating book in English too).

When translating Perquin it is important to reproduce her clarity without sacrificing too much of her lyricism and complexity. Stylistic features like rhyme and assonance should be maintained where possible, but not if their retention makes the passages in which they occur confused or cryptic. Striking a compromise between form and content is something of a balancing act and Perquin is a master at the gentle art of encouraging her translators to have another go, to try harder, to find that rhyme or pun. Often enough it was there after all, just waiting to be discovered.

Mother

The way she pipes up inside of you and has opinions,
butting in when you're talking, mostly uninvited,
get that hair out of your eyes, show your face,
do up those buttons, those sleeves look ridiculous
and can't you wear a scarf, it's windy.

The way she sighs in your breast
when you're at risk of buying something unnecessary, saying
sweet, fatty, bad for your heart, your liver, your blood,
the way she's hurt by booze and cigarettes, jaywalking
or reckless cycling – you're not allowed to die
or even get a fright or graze.

Like a slow-motion chase that lasts a lifetime.
She's on your heels. This progress forward,
one and two, in the same frame.

So often you fall short, so often you're okay. Always rescued
uninvited. Snatched away from dog and doorstep, fence and fate.
You look at her and don't know who she is.

Opposite: Ester Naomi Perquin, a woman with curly blonde hair tied back, wearing a collared shirt, smiles into the camera.

Care Advice

A girl is a peculiar kind of instrument: the harder
you hit, the softer her voice. Her body shrinks.
See the fine bones slip into their cells,
see the backbone wilt, the hesitancy
in those cutesy legs.

A girl will never be in the right place because she,
misplaced by nature, can't grasp the point. Not
anchored in this era, she slides off her chair
mid-conversation or simply disappears.

A girl is quick to fade. Sometimes she might have room
for a small collapsible self-image, sometimes
even a dream. As long as it's minuscule,
cut down to size.

Put a girl who opens her mouth next to a man's pronouncements.
Put a girl who wants something next to the will of God.
Put a girl who cries outside in the rain.
Girls don't break easily.

Just steer clear of romantics.
Girls don't thrive with them.
They make girls sick.

Contribution

Give a poet a war and they'll turn the blacked-out city
into a deep ocean. Shaping starfish from points
of impact, plankton from ash.

Fitting tanks with eyes and fins, rocking precarious façades
like kelp forests, constructing (for alliterative purposes)
coral reefs from stacks of skeletons.

The people, gasping for breath, half hidden,
eyes big and round –

Only a poet drives them effortlessly, as a single swerving school,
to safer water and admits, if asked, that it really is
just a poem, nothing more,

not bread, not oxygen cylinders, not education,
not protest, not a dividend, not a feat of arms,
not a wet suit, sporting event, peace benefit,

just talk, vague, under the surface,
largely inaudible, a poem

for every fish that's not yet lost.

A Nation's Prayer

Leader, wearer of medals, sharp as a wasp, great as a swarm,
who shines like the sun through the window of our screen, every pixel
refined, eloquent, millions of likes, millions of views,
everything we need to learn, we learn from you.

That this country shrinks if we remain silent, until it is
    no longer ours.
That we have right on our side.
That we are so right it shows in every family portrait.
That we are descended from justice (in a direct line).
That even birds, high and stateless, know our borders.
That our woods contain more trees.
That our water quenches better.
That our clouds are peerless overhead.
That we are proud, even when cowering before a blow.
That we can read and write better.
That we have been duped by history.
That the future will be very just.
That we are unique and therefore completely interchangeable.
That we have all been patient far too long.
That bullet wounds treated by our doctors often heal beautifully.

Father, custodian of reality, solid as a house, great as our capital,
teach us not to doubt when letting our sons and daughters go,
teach us to wave cheerfully at the window,
smiling at our progeny. Amen.

SAMBHUNATH CHATTOPADHYAY

Translated by Kingshuk Sarkar from Bengali

'Birds on a Banyan' is the English translation of the Bengali poem 'Botgache Pakhi' , from Sambhunath Chattopadhyay's 1972 collection *Rongin macher ghor* (A House for Coloured Fish). The poem also finds a place in the poet's *Best Poems* (1985).

The Bengali original is characteristic of Chattopadhyay's poetry – simple words, metrical perfection, a sharp well-defined image to hang the sense on, and an allusion to distance. Though 'Birds on a Banyan' is set in the urban clutter of Kolkata, many of Chattopadhyay's poems are set in distant lands ('Crane at Port Said', 'Curio Shop at Aberdeen Market'), in distant times ('Atilla's Stallion', 'At Tutankhamun's Tomb') or places which reflect distances. Death – a faraway place, both in time and space – is a recurring presence.

An obscure poet in his lifetime, Sambhunath Chattopadhyay now stands out among his contemporaries for his distinctive voice and technique. His poetry hinges on irony, something not common in Bengali poetry. An overarching philosophical sense (rather than wordplay), an impersonal tone and big pictures painted with a few strokes (rather than small intricate pictures of daily existence) marks him out. Unlike most Bengali poets, Chattopadhyay however is rarely political or social. He also happens to be one of those few Bengali poets who experimented with traditional western forms – villanelles, sonnets, etc.

The clear images and the universal themes of Chattopadhyay's poems make them yield to translations. His refreshingly modern poetic voice (preserved perhaps by his isolation and obscurity) appeals to a new generation of Bengali poetry readers.

Birds on a Banyan

The Banyan's canopy is dark,
heavy with the twitter of a million birds.
I stop.
It seems, the dark tree
is the disembodied voice of the dead
who used to wake up in this city
and with weary feet walked home every night
down these busy streets,
for whom the Jacaranda sunk roots
and bloomed on this concrete footpath.
They are here – their voices have become invisible birds' chatter.

Their tunes have merged into a symphony
deep inside the Banyan's mysterious canopy.
I walk to the tree, look up, and at once
realize: the shadowy tree
is the sad body
of an ancient violin.

JOSÉ KOZER

Translated by David Pollard from Spanish

'Master', said Reb Zaccai to Reb Dentè, 'you are a strange navigator. You explore the visible and invisible worlds claimed by the universe. And the ocean is ink for your pen.' It is an honour to work on the poetry of José Kozer. He was awarded the Premio de Poesía Iberoamericana Pablo Neruda (the Pablo Neruda Latin-American Poetry Prize) in 2013. I have translated a good deal of his work. I have some advantages and some drawbacks. The advantages are my Jewish background and study of Tenakh and being a JuBu which means I can pick up some of the Eastern references. I have also studied Kabbalah and spot some references there also. Plus the notion of exile which is crucial and which I love in the work of writers such as Jabès who, of course, fled from Egypt. In working on Kozer you have to go deep and swim in it. It is sometimes difficult to keep the arms and legs working as I have a strong sensation of wanting to drown. So many games to hide in his effort to hide what Jabès calls the Scream. You are forced on by the short lines for fear of stopping and being engulfed. You can't stop for fear of stopping. 'The impatience of the scream is its merit'. The swell or undercurrent alters the shape of the waves but is not seen there on the surface. You just keep on swimming. This is powerful stuff which I am gathering to myself, as I say. You keep at it, a poem a day because the writing allows you to keep swimming. I think I begin to understand this.

Fable 2

Please consider, with me, how I have escaped, even
without being pursued,
traveling over flat lands,
summer, the grass
high, thick green, I go at
the speed of the hare:
I haven't merely reached it but am back
in my lair, I count on
having what I need, the
squirrel and I both rest
(the hunter doesn't know
our galleries,
steps, detours)
long is the architectonic
dream (geometrical) that
conceals us in the burrow.

There is Kafka, where is God.

Lorenzo's labyrinths among the wounded ghosts of
García Vega, made of
earth, vilified,
just another in the same condition.
Leave off
panting.

Books, indiscriminate reading, raining, wind dying down,
the weather (furtive) stops
beating down, drifts,

the hunt devours,
consider with me,
There

is no
need
to go out.

All death, essentially, in the long run, goes
unnoticed. It lacks
introspection, being only
a repetition of words,
rhetoric, funerals (there is no
better convention):
air from air, earth always
virgin (fertilised) word
excrement, waste
of boards, fabrics, linings,
ribbons and crowns, first
the dead man is torn to shreds,
then the cloth, then the
woodworm preys on the
wood, the marble yellows,
gives way and collapses
and in the end
cracks. God cracks.
And slips away behind the classic
cloud that the ancient
Hebrews knew in their own flesh.

◆

I am a Hare, my shelter is real, it has two dimensions:
one room where the hare can
fret at his situation
the hare, nothing assaults it,
it doesn't jump, it lowers its ears,
regurgitates, stealthily
goes out, compelled by necessity:
returns, puts its affairs
in order and goes to the
window, sometimes real, sometimes
mental, and looks: he reads
anything and looks.
The grass is tall, the
greenery thick, ferns,
mushrooms, moss; it sniffs
the earth that harms it,
everything moves away, at his
shoulders two birds
cross a channel of
waters, their flight serene
(their reflections
calm: four
birds make up a
Universe, confirm it,
the hare between reflections,
considers how it
shows us busy and,
to a large

extent
absolved

OLGA ULTURGASHEVA

The Poetry Of Bargachan

The Eveny (Lamut) are one of the Tungus-speaking indigenous minorities (around 15,000 people) inhabiting the Arctic and sub-Arctic districts of Siberia. Eveny economy relies mostly on such subsistence activities as reindeer herding and hunting. These economic activities involving dependence on reindeer contribute to and still play a crucial role in the Eveny cosmology, rituals, and oral tradition. The extreme climate of Northern Siberia, characterised by minimalist ecosystems, long winters and freezing temperatures, has played a fundamental role in creating the unique artistic imagination of the community and its poetic imagery. But above all, Siberian Eveny poetry has been informed by people's everyday lives centred on human-reindeer relations and animist[1] beliefs.

Since Eveny poets have always responded to the events in their social universe, which included both humans and non-humans, the art of their poetry requires perceptivity beyond a lay person's normal capacity. Such perceptivity would connect a poet with the dimension of the sacred. Just like shamans the poets have always had a special connection with the domain of the ancestral and earthly spirits, and poetic gift has always been central to this connection. In Eveny oral tradition a poem has never been an artistic form belonging only to a genre of poetry, it was simultaneously a song, a dance and theatrical drama as, in addition to authoring the

1 Animism is a term used in reference to religious sensibility centred on a common mode of identification between humans and non-humans. Humans, animals, plants and material objects of social significance may be regarded as social persons or possessing human-like subjectivity. The understanding that all human and non-human components of the social universe are imbued with animate spirit or life force exists among almost all indigenous groups across Circumpolar North, Amazonia and Southeast Asia (see Brightman, Grotti and Ulturgasheva 2012).

poem, the poet had to be the author of a personal melody and choreographer of his/her own dance.

My father Vasily Bargachan (1941–2020), the Eveny poet and writer, was a living example of such multi-genre oral tradition. My first impression of him performing his own poetry comes from an image of him standing on a stage in a tiny community hall, crowded by Eveny reindeer herders who had just arrived to celebrate their traditional spring festival called Reindeer Herders' Day. Driving their reindeer caravans they travelled hundreds of miles along frozen winter routes from the farthest corners of the Verkhoyanye mountains to enjoy a concert of local artists, among whom was my father. Together with all members of the audience I, a five-year-old child, was mesmerised by the ways he read, sang and danced his own poem called *Khedje*[2]. Here is the poem that I translated from Eveny into English:

KHEDJE

In wonder, I gaze, can this be true,
Do elders dance as the young ones do?
Their steps so light, in the spring of their day,
Graceful as youths in their merry play.

Light as birds, in the sky so clear,
Or as dawn's light that the meadows cheer.
Like first snowflakes at morning's kiss,
Or fluffy seeds that the winds do twist.

2 *Khedje* is a traditional Eveny dance usually performed by an entire community. They dance in a large circle repeating in sequence after a lead singer. It is a collective dance during which a large circle of dancers imitates sounds of birds, animals, trees, wind, river and movements of reindeer that also tend to run in a large circle.

The cheerful leader calls the throng,
To see this dance, so bold and strong.
A sight of joy, of merry glee,
A dance that sets the spirit free.

Their hair may be silver, their years may be long,
But in their dance, they're forever young.
For in the Khedje's lively, whirling spin,
Age fades away, and youth dwells within.

I remember how the grace of his *khedje* movements and the energy of the poetic words enthralled the audience who, by the end of his dance, exploded with thunderous applause. It was one of his numerous performances that would always delight any audience. For example, his poems about spring would evoke hope and excitement about new beginnings brought by the blooming season. They were dear to any reindeer herder who always cherished the first signs of the arrival of a warmer season after nine months of extremely cold winter. Below is my translation of one such poem of his:

In the sun's vernal glance, coats fall with grace,
From shoulders they slip, like a warm embrace.
Till the break of dawn, in rapture, I'll be,
To listen to the stream's stuttering spree.

Birds' joyous chorus, the drip of the thaw,
And the scent of snow melting, fills me with awe.
Spring's lively clamour, to my ears, is dear,
It quickens my blood, brings the spirit near.

In harmony with the blooming, the earth so lush,
My soul, in tune, whispers a poetic hush.
Breathing out a verse, as light as the breeze,
Like a cloud tumbling, in the distant seas.

Since my father was a master of rhyme in the Eveny language, his best performances were always in Eveny. When the words of support were spoken from Bargachan's heart, they had a capacity to heal and restore people's hope. After my father's death an elderly Eveny reindeer herder approached me to say that: 'Your dad's words were such a remedy to my heart when I needed them badly. His supportive words gave me hope and literally healed me when I was in despair. I have nothing but gratitude for his poetry'. Given that Bargachan wrote mainly in his native language, he was saddened towards the end of his life to witness how the richness and beauty of the Eveny language started fading away, no longer being fully appreciated by younger generations of Eveny. But what I witness now is that, in search of their own voice, young Eveny draw their artistic inspiration from Bargachan's poetic imagery and the power of his rhymes.

Opposite: Vasily Bargachan, an Eveny man in a thickly furred coat and matching hood looks thoughtfully ahead.

ASWINI KUMAR MISHRA

Translated by Bibhu Prasad Padhi and Minakshi Padhi from Odia

Odia, one of the earliest languages of India, is largely spoken by the people of Odisha. The Odia script is the developed form of *Brahmi* having its root in Kalinga, the erstwhile synonym of Odisha. The state borders Bay of Bengal and provides a gateway for sea voyages to countries of southeast Asia. This, in a way, built up the seafaring strength of its people. In Odia literature this is reflected in several folk stories and poems, both in oral and written forms down the ages. Since the 13th century *Madala Panji*, the chronicle on palm leaves, Odia literature stretches across to deliver narratives on the Jagannath temple. The epigraphic testimony leads to the stone inscriptions available in western Odisha on the walls of Narasinghanath and Harishankar temples engraved during the fifteenth century. Two earlier books – *Sisu-veda* and *Saptanga* espousing Natha cult, Siva worship and Buddhism – appeared on the literary scene in the 13th century. The great epic *Mahabharata,* by Sarala Das, occupied the centre-stage during the 15th century as a masterpiece of socio-cultural wonder. For the first time, Odia plots and characters were textured in a brilliant manner.

In the 18th century Upendra Bhanj pioneered the cause of an ornate style in poetry. The 19th century gave rise to the experiments in romanticism through the verses of Radhanath Ray, Gangadhar Meher and others. In the 20th century free-verse yielded over, allowing Sachi Routray to pioneer. A few poets became loyal towards leftism including realism. Mysticism was relegated, allowing a humanistic spirit to be ushered in.

The White Hawk

For the last so many days,
For the last so many months,
It has not come down.
The news is not known
To the sky, nor to anyone else.

Perhaps, in the steaming heat
Of the sun, looking at
Its fiery wings,
We clap and say, 'Well, well'.
Don't flap your wings,
Be like a quiet kite
On the body of the sky,
Like the still boat
In the middle of the river Mahanadi.

The dancing raindrops
From the centre of the sky
Have not yet given up
Their search for
The white eagle's body.

The home-returning bird
Has asked some curator
Of the animal museum
To carefully maintain
A couple of wings.

Perhaps the two open wings
Shall come to life
In a birth of its kind,
Shall fly in the sky
Like some civilian aircraft
With a new name.

PRINCESS SHIKISHI

Translated by Seiji Hakui from Classical Japanese

All the poems translated here are written in the tanka form, a traditional form for short poems that follows the 5-7-5-7-7 pattern. But the form was not the only restriction imposed upon the poets then. As a custom, the tanka had to be written only in pure Classical Japanese with no Chinese loanwords, severely shrinking the vocabulary. In addition, the imperial court, the patron of literature, objected to any subject it deemed vulgar slipping into formal poetry. As a result, classical Japanese poetry almost always featured the same limited set of verbs, adjectives, animals, flowers etc. that the court culture approved of. For example, to say 'I love you' straightforwardly would be a faux pas. It had to be 'I think of you' or 'I miss you'. A poet may have seen some frogs hopping around in spring, but no, frogs were considered too vulgar to be in poetry. It had to be the bush warbler instead. Over time, the subjects allowed in formal poetry became instruments of symbolism.

A Summer Song

手にかをる
水のみなかみ尋ぬれば
花橘のかげにぞありける

Tracing the scent
Left on my hands,
Upstream I went
Till I found myself
Under the shade of an orange tree
In bloom.

A Late Summer Song

秋風を
雁にや告ぐる夕ぐれの
雲ちかきまでゆく蛍かな

Are you going to tell the geese
About the autumn breeze?
A firefly going up
Towards evening clouds.

FIONA SZE-LORRAIN

Interviewed by Jenny He

Fiona Sze Lorrain writes and translates in French, Chinese, and English. Her translations include Yu Xiuhua, Yu Xiang, Yin Lichuan, and Bai Hua. Her poetry includes *The Ruined Elegance* (Princeton, 2016) and *Rain in Plural* (Princeton, 2020). Fiona's latest work is the novel in stories *Dear Chrysanthemums* (Scribner, 2023), which is longlisted for the Andrew Carnegie Medal for Excellence in Fiction.

JH: Do you have a preferred place to work, or do you carry around notebooks to write as the inspiration takes you?

FSL: I see writing as a practice, not 'work' as a product or result of labor in terms of wages. I'm not taken in by the idea of an office as a factory that must yield output. Laboratory is more appealing to me.

I don't believe in productivity or a writing schedule. Artmaking is a mystery. It's organic and unpredictable. I don't carry notebooks not because they aren't helpful – quite the contrary – but that I don't wish to become a predatory writer . . . one who goes around stealing, jotting down, chasing – or worse, creating – experiences just to be able to 'use' them in writing. I've met writers who premeditate conversations in order to rack up lines for their dialogues in novels. It comes across as insincere to say the least.

JH: When you speak of a 'laboratory', do you think there is a 'scientific' aspect to writing? Can you expand on this idea more?

FSL: By 'laboratory', I mean the freedom to experiment and to work with the unknown. Trials and errors. Fail better, that is. Again it's the artmaking process – in this case, how a text is brought alive in another language, the relationship between the creator (both translator and writer) and the text – that matters most. Not necessarily the end product, and certainly not a 'commodity.' I generally find translations nowadays somewhat safe, streamlined, hygienic. So edited or revised that they rarely contain 'failures' that are interesting. In one of my *zuihitsus* 'Hand Notes from One Language to Another' (*The Poetry Review*, Spring 2022), I wrote:

'A Kunqu artist from Suzhou taught me to always make one meaningful mistake.'

JH: How do you feel when you have completed a translation?

FSL: A translation is never complete. Sometimes I leave something unsaid or undone. It's about leaving it in a soulful state of imperfection.

JH: The majority of the work you have translated is by women writers, was that a deliberate choice?

FSL: It wasn't planned. But through time I realize how vital it is to champion women writers and I haven't since regretted the path.

JH: Is there a difference for you translating the words of a man?

FSL: Of course. The voice is different.

JH: Do you feel that you channel a male voice, or does the translation become feminine in some way?

FSL: No rule of thumb exists. It depends. Once we try not to rationalise the mechanisms of translation, the issue of 'casting' fades away scrap by scrap. Translation is about translating IQ as much as EQ (emotional intelligence). In that sense, translation shares much with the craft of acting.

It springs to my mind that Czesław Miłosz and Leonard Nathan translated Polish woman poet Anna Swir in a collection that ironically carries the title *Talking to My Body*. Perhaps that isn't a paradox but a hint at the nondualism of translation:

> There are moments
> when I feel more clearly than ever
> that I am in the company
> of my own person.

This comforts and reassures me,
this heartens me,
just as my tridimensional body
is heartened by my own authentic shadow.

– Anna Swir's 'Myself and My Person' in Miłosz and Nathan's translation

JH: What attracted you to the work of Yu Xiuhua?
FSL: Her courage. I'd asked myself, What does it take to physicalise the act of writing? In particular, for a woman farmer suffering from cerebral palsy, living in poverty in a Communist, patriarchal society, surrounded by unforgiving people and circumstances?
JH: 'Crossing Half of China to "Fuck" You' is a very bold choice, but also the most appropriate. ('Fuck' works really well grammatically in the line). How did you get to that choice?
FSL: Thank you – I struggled with the word 'fuck', but I used it and had learned to accept it. There isn't any way around it: that was what the poet wrote. Clearly the poem generated a shock effect, but I find it useful to move past surface reactions about 'fuck' and not get distracted by its use, so to locate the 'bones' and vitality of the poem:

Half across China, anything can happen: volcanoes erupt,
    rivers parch
some neglected political prisoners and refugees
an elaphure and a Manchurian crane at gunpoint
I penetrate a hail of bullets to fuck you
. . .
I, as many, run as one to fuck you
Of course butterflies can lead me astray
and I think of some odes as spring

JH: What are the main challenges between translating from French and Chinese?

FSL: The main challenge involves the intensity of my listening. Partly because of its variety of composite sentence structures, French strikes me on occasion as domineering. Its musicality is seductive for lack of a better word. Chinese can be dry and hard on the ear, at times too curt, void of passion for my taste.

I'm not excited about the Chinese language in the 'touristy' way. It's been politicised.

JH: How does that effect contemporary Chinese poetry, and what part does translation and the translator play here?

FSL: It affects contemporary Chinese poetry in ways more significant than poets and readers might like to acknowledge: for example, abstruse or circuitous language that doesn't make sense except to create confusion and pass it for poetry because it 'sounds nice' and 'reads as sophisticated – I've come across such work in state-endorsed periodicals more and more often these days, even among the so-called established poets.

The history of politicisation in quotidian language creates distrust, mistrust, fear, which compels some poets to write 'for themselves' so to speak, in hope of resolving their own fears and contradictions through writing. But since that might not be possible due to censorship (including self-censorship), poetry in itself becomes a vehicle that creates more incoherence.

I'd say no to translating poems that promote moral and linguistic ambiguity, or exclude them from the poet's collection in translation if they don't represent the ensemble of the poet's writing.

JH: What were your earliest encounters with poetry?

FSL: I recall memorising Lewis Carroll's 'A Boat Beneath a Sunny Sky' and the first half of 'Grass' by Tang poet Po Chü-i for a class recital in Singapore at age eight. During rehearsals, I had to copy out both texts in a jotterbook multiple times.

I still continue to memorise poems, read them aloud. When I write, I write longhand and resist the stage of typing as long as I can. This is an important lesson to me: poetry is about making music; it is also the body.

JH: Do you memorise the poems you are translating, or copy them out in this form nowadays? Is this how you always work with the texts side by side?

FSL: Yes, I try to memorise poets I translate, at least a few of their short poems in the original language.

Translation isn't a form of photocopying.

I too don't work on my computer right away for translations. I work on paper. I've the Chinese texts before me and I write them out, verse by verse, in English on a fresh sheet of paper.

I email and surf online but I don't use mobile digital technology, in that I don't own a mobile phone. In short, I avoid seeing texts I'd translate on any screen for as long as possible. I want to experience poems, be they original or in translation, as words on paper first.

JH: Is it about a communication between the speaker and listener?

FSL: I like 'communication between the speaker and listener'. It evokes serendipity, the 'click' between a verse or an imagery and the reader. It suggests a literary friendship. The power of silence, even in words, is to me the essence of poetry. How do you write silence? This question is timeless and relevant.

JH: How is the process of translation different to your own writing?

FSL: What interests me in writing and in life is our humanity, what makes us more human and humane.

The experiences differ in balancing their pursuit of the mythic and the civic. I find translation time-consuming, poetry writing uncertain. We can translate anytime we want if we have a text, but not with poetry. Poetry is about waiting. It can also be about disobedience.

Translators are shadow heroines and heroes; translation is a thankless job. I agree there isn't enough recognition for translators.

Translators aren't authors in that they don't generate original contents, but they are the ones who bring alive a text in another tongue. I hope translators find opportunities to create more presence – not of themselves but of the text(s) – despite their invisible cloak. And for that to happen, they should be respected: credited rightfully, paid appropriately.

MARIJA DEJANOVIĆ

Translated by Vesna Maric from Croatian

The poem 'The Move', selected from the collection *Kindness Separates Night from Day* (Sandorf Passage, 2023), illustrates the style and the subjects characteristic of Dejanović's poetry. Her work conveys the relationship between space and identity. The question of origin reveals itself as the deepest and darkest source, and yet one that is also the most abundant and life-affirming. In Dejanović's poems, which could be classified as migrational literature, as well as ecofeminist, pacifist and postcolonial poetry, a singular female lyrical subject strips away layers of identity until she reaches a question, a wound, a sign of recognition and mutual understanding with those who dare search for answers to unsettling questions. Dejanović does not offer answers in her verse, but instead broadens her search and deconstructs all the common-sensical ideas about migrant identity, romantic love, the human and the animalistic, all the while questioning our possibility to code personal experience into language. Her lyrical subject is secluded even when it speaks in plural, and always connected to nature and society despite its permanent isolation. Dejanović questions the limits of patriarchal, (post)war, capitalist, consumerist societies by consciously rejecting the elusive promise of belonging.

Above: Marija Dejanović, a woman with dark hair, wearing a floral white dress, smiles softly into the camera. She stands in the woods, partially lit by a stream of sunlight to her left.

The Move

the moving of our organism happened
overnight

we threw off our fleshy armor
and forgot how to feel burdened

this didn't bother us much

the body vibrates as it lies by the lake

a water lily grows out of its ears
and its spine is an arrow
pointing south

where do colors go
when petals fall and return to the soil's embrace?

into your nose

they go into your nose

RABINDRANATH TAGORE

Translated by Adrija Ghosh from Bengali

In 2022, the National Centre for Writing granted me a Translation Residency to translate Rabindranath Tagore's *Bhanusingh'er Padabali*, a collection of 22 devotional songs written in Brajabuli, a mix of Sanskrit, Bengali, Hindi, Mythili, and Prakrit. These songs, depicting the love between Radha and Krishna, blend traditional Vaishnavite themes with Tagore's Modernist, Romantic, and Naturalist perspectives. The translation project explores Tagore's reinterpretation of the Padabali tradition, along with his diverse thematic approaches that highlight the clash of his spiritual systems, and linguistic fluidity. The translation process extends beyond linguistic conversion, incorporating my background as a Bharatnatyam dancer to infuse the text with a sense of physicality and sensory depth. By challenging normative interpretations and preserving gender fluidity inherent in the Padabali tradition, the poem in selection seeks to capture the nuances of the original text and serve as a testament to the richness of cultural hybridity, and the enduring relevance of Tagore's translingual oeuvre.

Beloved Radha, gaze upon Shyam who arrives
with tender steps and a tender song.
Hurry, adorn the flower garland –
Quickly wear your azure dress.
Fair maiden, take the vermillion
and decorate your fair head.

Friends, let us dance in joy
let us sing songs of reconciliation.
Let the melody of anklets clinking
fill the garden-grove. Beloved,
pour the ambrosia.

Light the golden lamp and fill the arbour
with the sweet scent of perfume.
Mallika, Chameli, Beli –
gather the flowers, maids
weave the wreath
of fragrant jasmine and malati.

With parched eyes, Bhanu heeds
the grove – the slow show
of Shyam approaching
with his tender tune and gait.

RAINER MARIA RILKE

Translated by Martyn Crucefix from German

Rilke's work tempts translators. This is a tribute to his astonishing skill with the German language, his boldness and mysteriousness as poet/thinker, and the creative frictions sparked between his German and our ever-changing Englishes. Unlike his sometimes more neologistic passages (in *Duino Elegies,* for example), Rilke's language in 'Tombs of the Hetaerae' has a fitting classical restraint.

The poem appears in the first volume of the *New Poems* (1907). Written while visiting Rome in 1904, Rilke had initially found the classical past, in 'the dead atmosphere of a dreary museum', preserved only as disconnected fragments. The opening 36 lines of the poem reflect this: a list of the bits and pieces found (in reality and imagination) in these particular ancient tombs. The hetaerae were courtesans in Ancient Greece. They were often highly educated and performed roles as artists, entertainers, and conversationalists, as well as providing sexual services. Alongside their teeth, like 'ivory figures in a travelling chess set', their ankle bones like butterflies, the 'silent crypt' of the women's sex seems but one of many details.

But in the second half of the poem, Rilke's syntax loosens and flows as he imagines their working (sexual) lives and the men and boys who were their clients. In a sustained metaphor, the women are now riverbeds, or the river itself, and sexual experience (the focus is on the women's, not the men's) deepens, broadens and elevates the individual. The poem's final lines suggest glimpses of a (Rilkean) sense of life's infinitude.

Tombs of the Hetaerae

In long swathes of their own hair they lie,
these earthen-brown, deep, and withdrawn faces.
Eyes closed as if from too much distance.
Skeletons, mouths, flowers. In their mouths,
the straight teeth arranged in tidy rows
like ivory figures in a travelling chess set.
And flowers, yellow pearls, slender bones,
hands and tunics, the decaying fabrics
over the caved-in heart. But beneath rings,
talismans, eye-blue stones (precious keepsakes),
stands still the silent crypt of the sex,
filled to its domed roof with flower petals.
And yellow pearls again, unstrung, let loose,
bowls of fired clay round the rims of which
are painted their own images, green shards
of perfume jars with the smell of flowers,
and statues of tiny gods: household altars,
the hetaerae heavens of charming gods.
Torn open girdles laid beside flat scarabs,
little figures sporting huge phalluses,
a laughing mouth, athletes, and dancers,
golden brooches that resemble tiny bows
for hunting bird- and beast-shaped amulets,
long pins, decorative household implements,
the ruddy ground of a rounded potsherd
on which run, like the black inscription
above a door, the stiff legs of a four-in-hand.
And flowers again, more scattered pearls,
the gleaming, curved limbs of a small lyre,

and, between the veils settling like mists,
as if just emerged from the shoe's chrysalis,
an ankle joint like a fragile butterfly.

And so, they lie, full to the brim with things,
jewels, valuables, toys, household goods,
broken trinkets (all that slipped into them),
and each growing darker like a riverbed.

And riverbeds they were –
above them, in short-lived, impetuous waves
(each wanting to progress to the next life),
tumbled the bodies of many young men,
and the streams of grown men surged through them.
And sometimes boys, escaping the mountains
of childhood, descended, in timid streams,
to play with what they found on the riverbed,
until its long incline was all they knew:

they filled then with smooth and limpid water,
spanning the whole width of this ample way,
with eddies, spinning, set in their deep reaches,
and for the first time they mirrored the banks
and cries of far-off birds while, high above,
night after starry night of a sweet land
flourished in skies that nowhere met an end.

VASYL STUS

Translated by Bohdan Tokarskyi and Nina Murray
from Ukrainian

These poems are taken from Vasyl Stus's first (illegally) published collection *Winter Trees* (Brussels, 1970). As Stus was a persona non grata after his public protest in 1965 against the arrests of Soviet Ukrainian intellectuals, his work stood no chance of getting past the censors. In *Winter Trees*, Stus gathered under one cover poems spanning the late 1950s–1960s – a crucial period in late Soviet history, marked by a shift from de-Stalinisation to a neo-totalitarian regime. Stus' poems reflect this turbulent transition. They show Stus as a poet of intensive self-reflection, playful irony, and masterly nature writing; they also serve as a scathing commentary on the oppressive post-Thaw period in the Soviet Union, and particularly Soviet Ukraine. Stus's fascination with trees is a running thread through his entire poetic corpus, which weaves together – in a jarring loop – streets, parks and forests in Donetsk and Kyiv with the landscapes of Kolyma. It was winter trees' austere essentiality that moved Stus to name his collection after them. While the powerful story of Stus's life has all too often obscured his immense lyric power, his poem 'The Model' warns us against a canonising reading of his poetry. In the mid-1960s, the sculptor Borys Dovhan approached the poet with the idea of creating his bust. Stus agreed, but insisted on looking down so that his gaze would not be captured. This was Stus's second experience acting as the model for a sculpture: Volodymyr Soroka made a bust of the poet in 1963. After that first experience Stus made a note in his journal that reverberates in 'The Model': 'I was scared, because my skin was taken off, I was made bare'. Evincing this introspection, 'The Model' serves as a reminder that far from being ossified, Stus's poetry resounds with scream.

The Model

Translated with editorial input from Uilleam Blacker

He is in despair.
He cannot rest inside himself.
Like a dripping candle, tear by tear,
he warms the sculptor's heart.
The artist takes life out of him,
he strips him bare –
nowhere to escape the hated eyes,
nowhere to find the fifth corner.
Oh, the mystery
of birth and dying!
These firm fingers
that took him
by the throat:
give all of yourself over
to the vicious cold eyes
of the other.
Malleable like clay
he fails
to find anything to cling to.
The dead body grows stiff
and now, membraned,
the model cools down
on a jagged note,
sharp as a spire.

My Head Is Weightless

My head is weightless
as if I'm slightly intoxicated
or as if
they had given me a general anaesthesia
and performed
a complete resection of my brain.
It feels good
after a whole day of hassle
to get into bed
like into a cold bath,
under the clean sheets
(they changed the sheets
in our dormitory today).
Feels so good to feel
this lightness in your head
and to know that nothing is bothering you.
(You'll have a good night's sleep?
You won't be troubled by insomnia,
will you? I won't count up to a thousand,
lulling myself to sleep
with my steady breathing?)
Dreams will be beautiful,
as upright as quiet rains.
I will stretch my body,
tired by a full day of errands,
standing in one line after another,
running to libraries and dates on the other end of the city.
I will come out of the deep recesses
of my here-and-there-and-everywhere-soul,

I will come free of the gears
of my spinning soul
and call:
'Come together now! There's no one else here,
just us!'
And all the parts of my body
will start coming back at midnight
like kind nocturnal fairies.
'Come together! It's nighttime!'
It's just me, there isn't anyone else.
Come,
so that by morning my mind would be charged again
by the million stimuli
from my sense organs,
so that tomorrow, refreshed, I could do it all over again –
the libraries, lines, and the dates on the far-off ends of the city.

BEARING THE BURDEN OF SAMENESS

Focus on Care

BRYNJULF JUNG TJØNN

Translated by Rachel Rankin from Norwegian

Brynjulf Jung Tjønn is a critically acclaimed, award-winning Norwegian author whose work explores the themes of adoptive identity, belonging, alienation and otherness. Discovered as a young child in Kyung San train station in the South Korean town of Gyeongsan, Tjønn spent his early life in Sung Rak Won children's home. At the age of three he was adopted by Norwegian parents and moved to Feios, a rural, sparsely populated village in Sognog Fjordane on the west coast of Norway. Despite having what can be described as a quintessentially Norwegian upbringing – being raised on a remote farm in an area of Norway known for its idyllic natural landscapes – Tjønn experienced and continues to experience racism and prejudice from those who do not consider him to be Norwegian enough. In 2022, Tjønn published the deeply personal poetry collection *Kvit, norsk mann* [White Norwegian man], which outlines and explores the racism and prejudice that he and many other adoptees in Norway experience, despite living in a country which is largely considered to be among one of the most equal societies in the world. *Kvit, norsk mann* was the highest-selling poetry book in Norway in 2022 and received the Norwegian Critics Prize (2022), the Norwegian Youth Critics Prize (2022) and the Nynorsk Literature Prize (2022).

These poems are taken from *Kvit, norsk mann* and feature reflections on adoption, Tjønn's early life in the children's home in South Korea, and experiences of shielding his young son from racism in Oslo.

ask anyone
and they'll say:
i want my own child
i want a child of my own flesh and blood
i want a child in
whom i can recognise
my own facial features
a child who other parents say
looks like its father or mother
i want a child who has my hair colour
my eyes, my nose, my chin, my cheeks
a child who reminds me of photos
i've seen of myself
from my childhood
and if i can't have that
i'll go through years of ivf
or travel to denmark
for assisted conception
and if i can't have that
i'll pay a poor woman in eastern europe or the usa
to carry my child to term

but someone
has to make do
with a recycled child
a second-rate child
a child nobody *really* wanted
a child surplus to requirements

i am the little child
without a name and birthday
without a mother and father
i am the little child
who aged two
was found in a train station
kyung san station
in the town of gyeongsan
and transported to
the children's home
sung rak won
in the same town
when i arrived at the children's home
i knew the korean words for
mum and dad

it says in my reports that i eat
a bowl of rice every day
and some vegetables and meat
and that my development is normal
and my physique is normal
i can take off my shoes if someone unties the laces for me
i can put on and take off my trousers by myself
it says in the reports that i like cakes, fruit and some snacks
i sleep from seven o'clock in the evening until six the next morning
i take a little catnap in the afternoon
it also says that i am *not cheerful*
i have *a gloomy expression*
i am fond of *one who cares about him*
puts out his arms if one holds him
it says that i don't play so well
with the other children
i would rather play by myself
it says that i like it best when i have a lap to sit on
i must be taken care of
with *abundant affection*

the glass door of the dentist's office opens
is minh here? asks a grey-haired dentist
is minh here? he asks again
this time he looks right at me
i look around and meet the dentist's
gaze again and shake my head
the dentist closes the glass door and disappears
what name did he say? i ask my son
minh, i think, replies my son
the dentist appears behind the glass door again
this time he doesn't open it
but looks through the glass
our eyes meet again
then he disappears
then another dentist comes out
she walks straight up to me
what's your name? she asks
i'm just here with my son, i say
oh, okay, she says and walks through the glass door
and i'm left sitting in the waiting room
thinking about minh
i picture a vietnamese man
a second generation immigrant
studying science at university
wearing high street brands
perhaps he is running through oslo city centre
late for his dentist appointment
perhaps it was a meeting that wouldn't end
perhaps it was a child who didn't want to go to nursery
perhaps it was a train that arrived too late
minh sprints sweating and stressed through oslo city centre

and doesn't know that the dentist thinks he's already here
that he's sitting in the waiting room
and that he doesn't understand much norwegian
that's why they have to ask him again and again
what his name is
but minh isn't minh
i'm the one who is there
i'm just here with my son
and the dentist thinks
i look like minh
and for a split second i'm relieved
that the dentist believed
that it was me who was minh
and not my son
that he avoided it
this time at least

RANAJIT DAS

Translated by Bidisha Mukherjee from Bengali

Born in 1949 to an immigrant family who took refuge in the Barak Valley region of Assam, India, as Bangladesh became increasingly unsafe for its religious minorities, Ranajit Das was the youngest member of the Atandra literary group in Silchar, Assam, at the age of fourteen. He moved to Kolkata in 1971 to find a place in his cultural homeland and live a poet's life. Das is noted for his distinctive style, not particularly reminiscent of his predecessors or contemporary poets in Bengali. An aesthetics of transparency marks his poetry as opposed to the aesthetics of obscurity found rampantly in the Bengali modernist canon. His poems are written in logically cohesive lines in a commonplace language while being deeply suggestive. The poems often end with a dramatic note of realisation, question or proposition, and some of his poems have a strong confessional flare. He also seems to have a preference for prose cadences and some of his finest poems are prose poems. In a number of his poems, we meet men from a generation that is slowly learning not to associate the tendency to care and nurture with femininity. In 'Sharmila's Loneliness' the poet-speaker is a man who has been taken care of all his life, and now he grapples with his inhibition while wanting to do the same for his woman.

Sharmila's Loneliness

My wife Sharmila is a lawyer. Every day before leaving for the court, she quickly eats a few morsels of rice alone. I notice it often. My retired life lets me stay in. By that time, I'd have finished the day's newspaper and it would be my time to sit in the balcony with the second cup of tea Sharmila would have prepared for me. It's just us in the house. She cooks, bathes, changes into her office clothes and then carefully fixes my lunch on the centre of the dining table. She tells me the day's menu and pleads with me to eat on time. Then she pulls a chair on a corner of the table, serves herself lunch, finishes eating with nimble hands and leaves for work. Day after day. Looking at her eating alone in the corner, I feel melancholic. But I never move close to her, I never ask, 'Sharmila, have some more rice. Take another piece of fish, why do you eat so little!' I don't, for it inhibits my male ego. These are things that Sharmila has asked me, our entire lives; as if it were a rule. I think her loneliness has begun ever since she married me. No one has fed her with care for these many years. Still, as long as her mother lived, once in a while she would be served with her mother's loving hands. But for a decade, she has lost even that last bit of care. She serves herself and eats alone. She will continue having her meals in complete loneliness for the rest of her life. Bemused, I observe Sharmila's lifetimes of loneliness at the dining table. And I wonder when I will be able to approach her and ask, 'Sharmila, here, please have a little more rice'.

XINYANG WU

Translated by Tuoya Wulan from Chinese

As a contemporary reinterpretation of the Chinese folktale 'The River Snail Maiden', the poem reflects on the exploitation of care and the precarious status of female agency. It is first inspired by a photo of snails as a popular street food in China. Fried and braised river snail reminds Xinyang Wu of the goddess who transforms into a river snail to save a farmer from leading a wretched life. The River Snail Maiden assumes human form, finishes all the chores, and returns to the shape of a snail before the farmer comes back home. After discovering her true identity, the farmer marries the River Snail Maiden. A discussion in the May Fourth Poetry Club around the wordplay of the character '坏' (corrupt, waywardness) further inspires the poet to rewrite the story into an allegory of modern love. By juxtaposing the eating of the snail with the taken-for-granted devotion of the goddess, Xinyang Wu questions the default kindness, labour, and sacrifice set for women in traditional imagination. 'Miss River Snail' dares to puncture the romantic bubble of predatory relationships instead of turning away to endure the suffering.

When I translate the poem, the image of gluttonous, emotion-predators waiting to devour a bowl of snails comes to mind. Instead of drawing the action of eating the snail's flesh, I wish to illustrate the cannibal nature of romantic connections that consume and imprison people in the name of love. One can rise to resist it as Miss River Snail does.

Miss River Snail

Brothers:
One less river snail eaten,
One more wife will be given.
The quality of the flesh,
Speaks her gentleness and devotion.

Haven't your hearts started itching?
Pity, the flesh won't keep,
Spoils when left in heat.

A spoiled snail turns into a wayward woman.
The fleeting shelf life
Dates her love
Bestowed upon you each.

Illustration by Tuoya Wulan

AILBHE NÍ GHEARBHUIGH

Translated by Billy Ramsell from Irish

Ailbhe Ní Ghearbhuigh, to date, has published three collections of poetry in the Irish language. Her most recent volume, *Tonn Teaspaigh* (*Heat Wave*), appeared in 2022 from Éabhlóid and was awarded the Oireachtas Prize for that year's best Irish language collection. Among her other prizes are the Michael Hartnett Award and the Laurence O'Shaugnessy Award. In 2016, the Gallery Press published *The Coast Road*, which featured translations of her work into English by thirteen of Ireland's leading poets.

A lecturer in the Department of Modern Irish at University College Cork, she has published widely on Irish language poetry and poetics, especially in the cross cultural and eco-critical contexts. A book of her translations into Irish from the French of the Egyptian-French poet Andrée Chedid were published in 2019 as *Dánta Andrée Chedid*.

Tonn Teaspaigh, the book from which 'Pressure' is chosen, triangulates itself elegantly between tradition and modernity, between the Gaelic past and a forbidding, fast-approaching future. 'Pressure', like the volume's other constituent poems, exhibits an inexorable rhythmic pulse, a crisp and tensile versification. It's a poem that progresses by jerking us from one startling visual to the next; images that are at times playfully dreamlike, that at times evoke a nightmarish unease. It's a text that enacts a profound and mounting anxiety, one maternal, ecological and very much of our time.

Opposite: Ailbhe Ní Ghearbhuigh, a woman with short blonde hair, smiles into the camera, holding her hands in her pockets. She wears a necklace and a black dress and poses against a thick expanse of leaves.

Pressure

So this is how it must be:
I live now in the kingdom of heat.

A child on the knee I can't budge,
her trace branded onto my thumbs

A red path has been burnt to my door
by ants, mice and visitors;

there's Gospel-pedlars to be gotten rid of,
the same with feathered invaders.

This fort is without protection
on my tree settles every obligation.

And in the time of craving it'll fall to me
to divide the very last morsel;

even bees will taste of that sparseness
for the season of want is approaching us.

What good's a good intention for recycling?
In my bag is a lump of dead batteries

and the cairn of nappies grows beyond measure.
To the dump with them and with everything!

In the ocean is a hillock of plastic
wth my daughter's name carved on its vastness

while on the wall there's a hanging barometer,
though I don't have sight of what's written there.

I married a man from these parishes
and when I did so I married the marsh.

I feel the ground give beneath itself,
in thick weather I can't breathe at all.

RONYA OTHMANN

Translated by Adam Tapper from German

When I saw that Modern Poetry in Translation was going to publish an issue on 'care', I thought of Ronya Othmann's haunting poem, '[nothing falls under this]'. Written from the dual perspectives of a caregiver and a hospitalised patient, Othmann deftly explores the intimacy inherent in caregiving relationships. As the poem opens, the caregiver-narrator laments the absence of her beloved in their shared bed. A few strands of the patient's hair cling to the pillows, enough to signal her recent presence but too few to make 'a wig' that might stand in for her physical body. The caregiver wishes for 'hospital | beds like ships', signaling the desire to escape their present state of suffering. At the poem's midpoint, Othmann initiates a shift in perspective and reveals the sacrifice both caregiver and patient have endured: 'i've given up | everything: arms, legs, torso, ovaries'. The next lines express the patient's anguish as she realizes that her caregiver is absent, 'her hands are not the ones that twist | and turn me'. Othmann uses sensory images to evoke the patient's longing. She closes her eyes to hear her caregiver's footsteps and the sound of her jacket 'flapping around her hips'. The yearning for this person, a source of comfort and care, is palpable. The poem concludes: 'now is not the time for | daisies', a flower regarded as a light-hearted symbol of joy and new beginnings. In giving the speaker(s) these final words, Othmann empowers them to express the gravity of their respective – and linked – situations.

[nothing falls under this]

nothing falls under this that i can write about in
january. her hair on
my pillow still doesn't make
a wig. i wish for hospital
beds like ships with white sheets, i've given up
everything: arms, legs, torso, ovaries,
and it dawns on me, drop by drop,
that her hands are not the ones that twist
and turn me. i search the blue
for signs. under my closed
eyes, footsteps, her jacket
flapping around her hips, a knock on the wood, the door.
now is not the time for
daisies.

ILMAR LEHTPERE

Translated by the poet from Estonian

In 2013 my wife Sadie Murphy was diagnosed with early-onset Alzheimer's. We were living in Estonia and it soon became very clear that Sadie needed to be in an English-speaking environment, so in early 2014 we moved to Birmingham. Her condition deteriorated rapidly and she was taken into an NHS Complex Care Unit, where she lived for almost six years until she was moved to a nursing home shortly before she died of Covid in 2020. I was with her all day every day throughout those years, doing most of the caring.

This is my English version of a poem from a long sequence of poems written during those six years which appeared in my collection *Kodutud luuletused*.

We are walking together
in the hospital corridor
You are holding my hand very tightly
I see that something is troubling you –
Your gaze is turned inwards
and your lips are moving slightly
You
poet
wordspinner
now have to seek out the simplest words
from deep within you
scrape them out
and then rehearse them
quietly to yourself

Finally you look at me
your eyes full of tears
and you say
Please always come and help me

CARLA NYMAN

Translated by Beth Hickling-Moore from Mallorcan Spanish

Carla Nyman's 2023 collection, *Líquida tuya y vertebrada* ['Your liquid and vertebrate'], explores a radically real and scandalous type of love, presenting a correlation between sexual desire, intimacy and the physiological.

Nyman's emphasis in 'Líquida' is on the sonorous and scatological: it is a celebration of the corporeal in all of its flesh, filth and excreta, examining and lauding the individual body as well as what happens when one encounters another. Yet for all of its initially repugnant onomatopoeia and visceral descriptions, Nyman's work is startlingly intimate: each poem contains a longing to know, feel and taste the body, to the degree that she longs for hers to amalgamate with that of another.

Beyond the blatant physicality and sexuality evident in these poems is also the underlying sense of care, 'unconditionally loving all of your primary functions', 'warmly withstand(ing) the weight of decomposition' while 'hand in hand' or 'nestle(d) inside your muscles'. This type of care is not the type that often features in poetry; it is strangely intimate and even romantic in its unsavouriness.

The delight and difficulty in translating Carla's work is her attention to sound and onomatopoeia: the use of assonance, sibilance, invented compound words and unusual spellings which emphasise the corporeal quality of her work. I spent some time sitting at my desk, exploring the possibilities of sound and texture in my English translation. All the while, I rolled the words around on my tongue. I encourage you to read them aloud, too.

and i try to keep you inside

upwards

and downwards

unconditionally loving

all of your primary functions

putting your skeleton upright

and there where we merge

i'll be able to take your fffibres

lift yourrr kneecaps your navel

traverse imprudently

until I get to your pith to bre-ak it

And excitedly nestle inside your muscles.

◆

what do I know

the heaviness of dragging a body taking a body a
long

time

what else to say

if it goes about also lying with an other(s)

bearing unnatural positions

beaten by this new way of getting up

three metres of liver up to the decrepit

intestinal taste

this is a coordinated tourist

one who measures their excess weight

with the divine colossal

fat of another

is there someone outside?

fantastic disgrace of living;

breaking itself in contradiction

towards the thing it loves

how to pose from within

my limbs on others

letting my body fall

mitochondria and movement

landing on you.

I have recognised

your position on the exact axis of your perpendicular existence

if I were there

if we were an organism

body mass and entrails duplicated

with these we would be

withyou more withme than ever

withus all matter

diluted into only one: puddle of piss and faeces

let's confuse each other love each other devour each other

to fill our mouths with the same substance

DESIDERIO DESIDERAVI HOC
PASCHA MANDUCARE VOBISCUM!!!

think about it we would go
hand in hand all day

earwax lymph and aorta

yoursandmine

to warmly withstand

the weight of decomposition

think about the jubilation

there is no love another form of fallinginlove

there is no love another form of fallinginlove

mybody is gloriously pisssoaked love

yourbody is gloriously excremented love

◆

me with you inside after

simply walking together

through the streets

we will see all the people

passing by us

saying hi while

i tightly squeeze your pancreas

so that it is mostly

ridiculous

that you shoot glances

you never dedicate to my body

so secret

let's love the living while they're living

i'll tell you

but you and i! listen:

matched up always

stomach-lover

this will be our love our cadaver

who am i

a succession of unlovings

tangled with the gastric body

Above: Vivian Lamarque, a woman with shoulder-length hair and glasses smiles into the camera.

VIVIAN LAMARQUE

Translated by Vilma De Gasperin and N.S. Thompson
from Italian

The four poems here are from 'Poesie ospedaliere' ('Hospital poems') in the collection *Madre d'inverno* (*Mother in Winter*, 2006), and refer to the poet's adoptive mother who died in December 2008. The poet addresses her mother, remembering loving and slightly awkward gestures, but also the affectionate exchanges during the last days of her life, acts of care that bring no relief to the mother's pain, nor distract the poet from the looming loss, but testify to the profound bond between mother and daughter.

In spite of its familial and dialogic tone, Lamarque's poetry conceals surprising complexity. Her poems often stem from quotidian gestures, which she imbues with startling depth.

For Those Who Have Watched Over A Mother's Bedside At Night

Far from the vision of the immaculate
peaks of the Himalayas, far from the wonders
of volcanos in renewed activity, far
from a site to observe the majestic
Falls in the film *Niagara*

the vision of a pure white slope appears
as I watch at the site of your hospital bed – the sheet
that tortured breathing lifts
and falls, lifts and falls, the embroidery trembles
on the white gown, a mother-of-pearl
button shudders in precarious equilibrium,
the thermometer gleams quite still
placed on the bedside table
like a dawn or a sunset, the rose
of the drip feed and the gold
of the urine sack and the white shawl forms the slope
covered in snow so much snow in fact
you're struggling to utter the words can you feel
how cold it is here how cold it feels?

The Positions Of Pain

Why could they never find the veins?
Why would they blotch your snowy arms like that?
And I could never find the nurse
to ask her and visitors
never found the room to visit
and you never found the remote control,
even though it was there, that raised
the bed so that every two hours
the positions of pain could be changed.

Hospital Jealousy I

You didn't like it if I spoke
to the person in the next bed
even less if I straightened
her pillow or poured her a glass
of mineral water or passed her
her cell phone.

With your great fearful hands
you clutched me
pulled me closer, you once had
so little, poor thing,
that you were jealous of a neighbouring bed.

Hospital Jealousy II

And idiot that I was
I divided my time on my visits between you
and the plants of the whole unit
that I secretly watered, between you
and the Christmas decorations that
like someone possessed I'd hang up everywhere,
and how jealous you were, and how right.

CĂTĂLINA FLORINA FLORESCU

Translated by the poet from Romanian

If what we saw in front of us was the only true and real world, we would be so poor! Luckily, we have imagination and dreams. We have losses and pains. We have friends and enemies. We have days of hunger and days of lust. We have words that come easily out of our bodies and minds, and words that are too shy to face the world and want to be only with us. At least for a while. Do not rush them. Do not rush yourself.

The poem is simply what I wrote above. When I translated it from my adoptive mother tongue into my birth language, the activity was just as natural as drinking water on a hot summer day. Meaning, unlike my first years in the US when translation was synonymous with homesickness, the two languages have finally decided to co-exist peacefully. Through this poem, I invite others to continue it because whether or not you are mono- or multilingual, a writer or a mechanic, a teen or a senior, you have dreams that await to be freed into the world. Do that. Not for me. Not for you. But for your dreams.

Above: Cătălina Florina Florescu, a woman with wavy hair, takes a selfie, holding a peace sign. She wears a black top with a heart containing a wreath of flowers.

'To Be Continued...'

Imagine a hand. It is in front of you
reaching out.
Imagine a pair of scissors
that cuts papers
anticipating
the next holiday.
Imagine an equilateral triangle
bearing the burden of sameness
knowing that that was possible only
in geometry –
That life is strife
and light
and poorly cut out shapes
and that you
of all people, *you*
are awake:

Imagine that.

Above: Ishita Baduri, a woman with dark hair and glasses, speaks into a microphone.

ISHITA BADURI

Translated by Mamata Nanda from Bengali

Ishita Bhaduri is an important voice in contemporary Bengali literature. Born in a family of highly respected poets and poetry lovers, she began writing at a young age and now writes poetry, rhymes, short stories, essays and travelogues. There are 44 published books to her credit, including a poetry ebook. She has been praised by reviewers for her acute observation of life, superb artistry, vivid imagery and a perfect sense of a good ending with complete absence of gimmicks. Her poems have been translated into English, Russian, Spanish, Romanian, Taiwanese, Hindi, Oriya, Rajasthani and Gujrati.

In the last few years, a destructively virulent virus has threatened the very fabric of our lives, as it spread and multiplied across the world. Then came the added burden of wars and natural disasters. They increased the sense of our own mortality, our human frailty and our powerlessness. The upside of living through such horrific experiences is our realisation that we all have more strength and resilience than we are aware of. In periods of tragedy and disaster, there can be a sense of pulling together, of looking out for one another and of offering a helping hand to those who are particularly vulnerable. Ishita addresses all this in her poetry with tenderness and optimism. In 'When All This Is Over' she expresses how the period of social distancing reminded us of the importance of some of the simple pleasures in life that we normally take for granted – being in the company of loved ones, sharing small achievements with fellow human beings, performing seemingly insignificant day-to-day activities. In this poem she celebrates those moments in a way that is universal.

Two notes to the poem: Connaught Place is the heart of Delhi. It is the ultimate place to experience the vibrant nightlife of Delhi, and houses many ['almost all' begs a big question] famous international chain stores, famous food chains, rastaurants and bars. Marine Drive is a three-kilometre-long, banana-shaped, six-lane concrete road along the coast of a natural bay promenade in Mumbai, India.

When All This is Over

When all this is over, I'd take mother to the hillside on an aeroplane and get close to the clouds.

When all this is over, I'd sit on the floor and tear apart the days and nights of illness. I'd hold 'social distancing' in my hand and smash it into fragments.

When all this is over, I'd sit on a moving train and run past the darkness to see the flickering lights. I'd break wild waves in the black sea with you.

When all this is over, we'd gather together at the junction of the highway and ceremoniously burn the masks. We'd hold hands and see all the faces.

When all this is over, I'd swim in the river Ganges all the way from the holy town to the banks of the megacity. The rainbow in the sky would scatter its colours into your eyes . . .

When all this is over, I'd eat caramel pudding in the old confectionery in Connaught Place. I'd take a walk with old friends in the Marine Drive in Mumbai.

When all this is over, I'd unlearn the word pandemic. I'd get the rosy dreams out of the locker and stare with yearning eyes . . .

SAIF ANSARI

Translated by Ashish Kumar Singh from Hindi

I came across Saif's poetry while scrolling through the PoemsIndia website. There, he had four poems that I read and then reread. I was both fascinated and astounded by his ability to weave so effortlessly the human aspect with the natural world. He writes with the simplicity and lyricism often associated with Mary Oliver. I knew I had to at least try to translate them. And since I had never translated anything before, I had no idea the struggle that lay before me. I have tried my best to capture the essence and beauty of the original Hindi poem as closely and accurately as possible.

Why Didn't It Die?

One winter night,
I touched a tree,
its trunk had gone cold.
Why didn't it die of coldness?
Leaves it has shed,
but dry it has not.
Why didn't it die of coldness?
Then, I looked
on the ground
at the web of its roots
and at a similar tree
that stood
in front of it.
I thought, maybe somewhere
below the ground,
they held each other
by their roots
like we do to someone
in their grief, and this,
I learned from the trees!

ŞAFAK SARIÇIÇEK

Translated by Csilla Toldy from German

I met Şafak Sarıçiçek virtually, through a dialogue organised by UNESCO City of Literature Ulyanovsk. I was interested in his poetry because of his bilingual heritage. Born in Istanbul, he has a Kurdish linguistic background, while he has written six books of poetry in German. In 2023, I was awarded a scholarship by the UNESCO City of Literature Gothenburg and spent a month translating his collection, *Comets Comets*.

In his poetry, Şafak Sarıçiçek draws the picture of an anthropocentric world, in which humans are lonely, restless, separated from each other and their environment. People searching for comfort and security, for an insurance against their own mortality, merged into masses, in submission to autocracies.

Eco-poetry or environmental poetry coming from German-speaking Europe is rare in the English language. Şafak adds a deeper dimension to it, drawing on the mystical from his Kurdish/Zazaki origins. A language that is slowly becoming extinct finds expression through his use of German that the translator intends to express in English, like in *20mg lyrical antidepressant*, full of energy and positivity. In Şafak's words:

'As many psychiatric prescriptions contain milligrams of an active substance, this poem from the tradition 'konkrete Poesie' contains the image of a small poem that lives and contains 20 mgs of euphoria. No serious side effects are known.'

Opposite: Şafak Sarıçiçek, a young man with curly, dark hair, smiles into the camera. He has stubble and wears a checked shirt, holding a bag over his right shoulder.

20mg lyrical antidepressant

this is here a colossal anti
depressant, splendid laughter, positive
mood liquefied in the canister of a printer cartridge and
from there onto this note that you hold in your hand, this is here
optimism, an explosive mix of elevated mood and motivation thrust
made of letters:
YOU ARE FANTASTIC and PHENOMENAL!
IT'S GOOD THAT YOU EXIST!
This is here a colossal anti
depressant, a lyrical, 20mg,
sealed for you into this phial.

ABDULLAH O. JIMOH

Translated by the poet from Yoruba

These poems are my work, both the first versions in Yoruba and the translated versions in English language. Being an exophonic writer, the creative process in my writing involves the processing of two languages (my mother tongue and the language with which I mostly write, English). Also, being a linguist, I find it interesting to translate from my mother tongue to English and vice versa. Poetry, though it is more of oral form, flourishes in Yoruba culture too. In the language, it is known as Ewi. Yoruba language has its idiosyncratic features such as tone system, sentence structure, syllable structure, vowel harmony, and so on.

These poems are written to account for the theme of care as observed in the Yoruba community. The poem 'My Brother' concentrates on the exchange of attention between kids. The construction 'Ọmọ Ìyámi' in Yoruba literally translates to 'my mother's child' but the phrase is not in all cases used to mean my mother's child. It is a common slang among the youth which means 'My Brother', figuratively denoting a peer, a friend, or a companion and this is what it means in this poem. The second poem 'The Garden Must Tend Me' centres on self-care. It is like a recitative affirmation. Hence, the personification of 'Ọgbà' (Garden) as in 'Ọgbà gbọ́dọ̀ tọ́jú èmi nàá' (Garden must tend me too). The word 'Tọ́jú' in Yoruba translates 'to look after' which is a phrase that is synonymous with the word 'tend' as used in the poem.

Overleaf: Abdullah O. Jimoh, a man with very short hair, takes a selfie. He has a backpack slung over his left shoulder. Behind him, we see a series of concrete buildings.

My Brother

I had a ball & a bicycle back then
and can't play or ride all alone

so I shared my self with you
and you did the same with me.

We were about seven years old
when I learnt about brotherhood

but it was not from school,
it was from you.

I called you my brother, even though
you were not my blood. We youngins

have redefined family as people not
related by blood but by love.

As a kid trying to evade boredom,
I was busy, looking for the seed of fun

on the pitch. You, looking for it too,
saw me. We synergized and found it.

We planted it and it bloomed.
& later we sat under its tree,

the shade covered us
and protected our friendship

from the burning touch of the sun
as we enjoyed each other's company.

The Garden Must Tend Me

Last week, I did not attend jumu'ah
because overthinking numbed my strength.
Today, I flush tablets of hope down my throat
with water and attend jumu'ah. I must not allow
the chain of the past tether me like an anchor
clasping a ship. I must rise up everyday with
daybreak in the garment of the sun. I must shine
to light up my dark world. I must burn the shrub
of my aches and play with the cinders. My worries
are feces, each time I visit the toilet, I flush them
down the closet. Henceforth, I will not be
the only one tending the garden, the garden must
tend me too. I deserve joy, warmth of sunlight,
and the coolness of water too. I deserve weeding
away my sorrows to let in fresh breeze into my
presence. I must make care scent in my ambience.

ADRIANA LISBOA

Translated by Alison Entrekin from Brazilian Portuguese

Adriana Lisboa is one of Brazil's foremost novelists and poets, and a master of subtlety. I've been translating her work for many years, but I still find it tricky to tease out the meaning of her poems with the same economy of language. I don't want to bloat them with expansionist explicitation; rather, I want them to be compact and cryptic as they are in the original.

Take, for example, the verses 'none of this exempts me | from certifying the signature of my footsteps'. The original in Portuguese uses the phrase, *reconhecer a firma dos meus passos* which is literally 'recognising the signature of my footsteps'. But *reconhecer firma* also means 'to have a signature notarised'. This speaks of an awareness of the marks we leave (on earth? on others?), but without being so explicit. Luckily, I was able to do something similar with 'certifying', which is a different verb but strikes a balance between two possible readings, one of which maintains the notarial reference.

The verses *o fato de as palavras | falarem por si e pelos cotovelos* were amusing. The expression *falar pelos cotovelos* (to speak through one's elbows) is like 'to talk the hind legs off a donkey' in English. But it would have inflated the line too much. I also wanted something that could be used with 'speak' without needing to add an extra verb. 'Nineteen to the dozen' fit the bill nicely.

To A Friend Who Is Waiting

The fact that I am all
emptiness
and that not even
of the shadow of an atom undone can it be said
            that it's that and not something else

the fact that I'm perched
atop a world headed for ruin
for all that we've been sabotaging it for
all that we've been corroding the skies
and decimating the living

the fact that words
speak for themselves and nineteen to the dozen
            (just open
            the floodgates to their concrete lexical fury)

none of this exempts me
from certifying the signature of my footsteps
            the same ones that go through the neighborhood
            down the wide avenue
while a tattered angel sticks me with
two dagger eyes

they've given me a name   a roof even
I've gone about peddling a half dozen verses
I've exercised inadequacy in so many ways
always in pursuit of that which always recoils (hence
the metaphors)

the fact that it's all marsh
light   and the sun
an indifferent star
the fact that I'm even unlearning
my shyness (having concluded that
it too is immodest)

none of this exempts me
from the flood of the moment
from taking to the streets against the intolerable
from clearing the weeds that threaten the gerberas
from waiting a few seconds
          before
pouring freshly-boiled water
onto the ground coffee

to then serve the coffee
to a friend who is waiting

REVIEWS

How Can I Keep My Heart Whole?

Nostalgia Doesn't Flow Away Like Riverwater, by Irma Pineda, translated by Wendy Call, Deep Vellum, 2024

Review by Robin Myers

Anyone who has ever left home comes to understand that they are changed by the act of leaving – and that the home they return to, if they ever return, is as vulnerable to transformation as they are. The path is strewn with questions. What if they change so much that they truly lose what they've left? What will happen to their loved ones who stay – and what will become of their love? How long is too long to return? Will nostalgia conserve or corrode?

Of course, not all departures are created equal: one thing is to relocate by choice, and another is to be pressured into migration by economic hardship, climate crisis, and ecological devastation. These are some of the undercurrents running through *Nostalgia Doesn't Flow Away Like Riverwater*, by prominent Binnizá (Isthmus Zapotec) poet Irma Pineda, translated by Wendy Call. In a three-part collection of persona poems, one speaker leaves the town of Juchitán, Oaxaca, and travels to the United States as an undocumented labourer; their partner, the second speaker, stays behind, awaiting their return.

Structurally, *Nostalgia Doesn't Flow Away Like Riverwater* is a smooth and solid vessel: each of the three sections contains twelve poems interlacing the voices of the two speakers as they ruminate to themselves and invoke each other. In the first part, the migrating partner weighs the decision to leave and the trials ahead; the remaining partner considers the pain of their beloved's departure. In the second, the partners converse through metaphors of place, navigating the migrant's sense of loss and alienation from afar. The third and final part intensifies the migrating partner's anguish of separation – and their fear of returning empty-handed – while also emphasising their beloved's steadfastness in the hope and joy of reunion.

Inside these firm structural parameters, the poems have a fluid, expansive sense of motion. There's something water-like about how they shift, dilate, ebb in space and time: we never know exactly who the speakers are or where the one who migrates has gone to; we don't know how long they're apart; we don't know much about their partnership other than that they love and yearn acutely for each other. It's this deliberate and evocative open-endness that allows the poems, too, to absorb other separations, struggles, and subjectivities; to probe the relationship between individual decisions and communal history and circumstances. In Pineda's words, as quoted by Call, 'I create poetry as a way to keep collective memory of my culture alive and to reflect on what is happening to our culture. When I say "our culture", of course I'm also referring to the earth, to the sea.'

Needless to say, water imagery is central to this thematic expansion. Throughout *Nostalgia Doesn't Flow Away Like Riverwater*, the ocean is omnipresent as a source of nourishment and livelihood for Isthmus communities – including and especially when that sustenance is lost to the ravages of pollution, exploitation, and climate change. 'The sea stopped birthing fish and now vomits rusted cans', reads one poem in Part II; '...The sea went deaf and tossed us | into the desert's arms | The sea went deaf and hurled us | onto someone else's path'. In images like these, the ocean appears not only as a site of material and cultural significance, but also as a being of its own, complicated and alive: an independent force with both generative and destructive power. Throughout the book, nostalgia itself swells, surges, and multiplies, vast and insistent as a sea. 'Nostalgia doesn't melt like water underfoot', we're cautioned by the poem that lends the book its title: 'Nostalgia doesn't flow away | like riverwater | but becomes a sea | that pulls at us relentlessly'.

Pineda writes in both Spanish and Didxazá (Isthmus Zapotec), which means that both iterations of her poems are the originals: she calls them 'mirror poems'. In a wonderful translator's note that opens the book (a trilingual edition), Call describes the process of translating these two poetic traditions into English as 'negotiating a series of border crossings'. A word like 'nostalgia', for instance, presents two paths: one is the Spanish 'nostalgia' (which hews closely to the English conception of the same word), while the other is the Didxazá 'xilase' (which is more like melancholia, a state of physical malaise induced by emotional anguish). The paths fork. Here, Call chose the Spanish path; elsewhere, she opted for the path marked by Didxazá. In this sense, the richness and capaciousness of the poems themselves – their subjective undulations and temporal indeterminacy, the prismatic nature of 'nostalgia' affecting and transforming both the person who leaves and the person who stays – is also borne out movingly in Call's translations, and in the collaborative spirit between author and translator that has shaped their work together for many years.

A translator as sensitive as Call knows – and shows – that once she embarks on a 'path' set by a word, phrase, concept, rhythm, or sonic texture in a source language, the path she forges in English will lead her somewhere entirely new. I love the moments of her translation when she revels in the music of her own making. For instance, in the poem 'This Path' from Part II, she follows a parallelism present in both Didxazá and Spanish and intensifies its reiterative effect with alliteration richer and more emphatic than what we find in the originals: 'The lights twinkling from the river's far side | dazzle | dizzy | deceive'. In another delightfully sonorous image from Part II, Call's enjambments work wonders in accentuating consonance and slant rhymes: 'Since you left | our sliver of sky | is starless but sometimes | one star gleams and becomes / more brilliant...'' There's nothing gratuitous about these accentuations, and they don't sparkle for the sake of sparkling; they do the work, as any poem must if it's truly alive, of animating what the words would otherwise simply say. In a poem and in a collection that explores the enduring love between two people separated by a vast distance, as well as the terrible intimacy of the fear and hope each nurses alone, Call's English finds its own pauses and textures, its own breath, to capture the fluctuations of their longing.

'If I go back', the migrating partner ventures in Part III: 'it will hurt to hold in my hands | all that I discovered here | How can I keep my heart whole?' And in the next poem, their beloved back home replies:

> The day will come
> when I can gaze at your face
> although it will be only part of you
> that returns to us
> it won't matter if you return empty-handed
> we will embrace you.

In the end, *Nostalgia Doesn't Flow Away Like Riverwater* offers solace and faith in the abiding strength and warmth of this 'we' and its embrace – but it never looks away or minimizes the painful reality of what has been lost. After all, Pineda's book does tell a story of loss, or many stories of many losses. A person is wrested from home and confronts new forms of vulnerability and isolation. Another person grapples with their absence and confronts the very forms of precariousness and destruction that led their beloved to leave in the first place. A culture and an ecosystem respond to ecological crisis, mass migration, and other convulsive changes. Neither love nor nostalgia suffices to spare them the pain and uncertainty of these transformations, in the sense that every loss is always a transformation, too. But they affirm, again and again, the power of the personal and communal bonds that weather it, spiraling through time and space with the suppleness of a nautilus shell. Whole or not, the heart beats on, exultant and embraced.

I've Read Everything You've Ever Written

Living in Language, ed. by Erica Hesketh, Poetry Translation Centre, 2024

Review by Chloe Eliott

> The poet recognises something in her writing when, in saying 'I', she feels she is uttering a voice that is both close and, at the same time, distant. She feels she is translating into herself something that seems to come from far away in time.

These are the words of Diana Bellessi, written in a letter to Ursula K Le Guin, translated by Leo Boix. What does it mean to write into the body? When we write 'I' we are externalising the self, as we are taking it in. The action follows a movement of breath, expelling air, as we go on, to encompass it. How do we bring the 'I' closer? As translators, we receive the 'I', holding it as close as we can to ourselves. We feel the shakiness of its breath, its impossible gestures and the urgency of its speech. Bellessi, an Argentinian poet who has become one of the foremost voices in Latin America, and Le Guin, a renowned American speculative fiction author, poet and essayist, acknowledge translating each other as a way of fostering cross-cultural dialogue. They exchange the 'I' in the most intimate of senses. As Anton Hur writes in an interview published in Scroll.in, 'The match between translator and a writer is alchemical. It's like being in a marriage'. We see this reciprocal relationship; in an October letter, Bellessi leads us through a sleepy Sunday morning, guiding Ursula through the trees that surround her house. She writes,

> I see the first greenery emerging, delicate filigree, almost invisible, and their magical, extraordinary growth, in wreaths of leaves whose variety never ceases to amaze me. Let me name them in my

language: fresnos (ash trees), arces (maples), plátanos (plane trees), paraísos (paradises); they are the ones that abound in the streets, and suddenly a (tilo) lime tree, a Judea tree, the aura of a sauce (willow).

She gifts Le Guin language, but also a landscape, a tilting forest of thought, inviting her closer. As readers, we are awarded a tenderness, a glimpse into an exchange that has been going for 15 years. These are love letters worthy of Frida Kahlo and Vita Sackville-West, Bellessi declaring, 'I've read everything you've ever written, did you know that?' It's a translation relationship that relies on closeness and trust. We feel that these are two women who carry each other's words with them wherever they go, make them part of their bodies, bring them to Napa Valley and a museum in Berkeley and the Forest itself.

It's this exchange that sits at the heart of Poetry Translation Centre's (PTC) *Living in Language*, edited by PTC Director Erica Hesketh. The compendium brings together reflections on the composition and purpose of poetry and translation from 22 poets around the world. We're awarded lyric essays, fragments and poems that reflect on craft and vulnerability. The pieces speak to each other, just as Ursula and Diana do. In Habib Tengour's 'Embracing the Gnarled Ineffable', translated by Delaina Haslam, poetry is understood as a destabiliser to myth, whilst in Diana Anphimiadi, translated by Natalia Buka Peters, we learn of heroines – Clytemnestra, Pandora, Cassiopeia – as characters that help us navigate a modern world undercut by violence, war and patriarchal convention.

Poetic form is also approached by Karan Kurose, translated by Alan Cummings, in an essay that highlights the Japanese tanka. Readers are introduced to 8th-century iterations of the tanka:

The snow
That lies on Mount Tateyama
Even in midsummer

I never tire of gazing upon it
Surely this is a sacred mountain

Here, Ōtomo no Yakamochi, an 8th-century aristocrat, gazes in awe at the scale of the world above him, contemplating the sublime. Kurose pulls us in, revealing a 'chimeric language' that is multiple historical periods at once. We witness its origins, just as we feel its contemporary shift, pulling us 1,300 years forward like a 'tidal current'. Kurose shows us his own tanka, this time gazing over the white cliffs of Dover.

'Big water!'
My child laughs out
Holding her to my chest
And walking along the shore
Till she grows up a little

The form, like the classical poem, follows the tanka's 5/7/5/7/7 format. The sublime is still present, but this time has been distilled to something more playful and tender. The sacred is now at arm's reach. The magnitude of emotion remains, though perhaps we feel the tanka more deeply, its pendant-like shape like a small thing we hold to our chest.

Elsewhere, in 'A Poem on My Gravestone: On Death, Being Minang, and First Love', by Indonesian writer Zar Mose, translated by Khairani Barokka, we see the exclusion of queer and ill bodies. We understand that safety is not felt equally. That writing, in the words of Víctor Terán, is a form of defence against oblivion. Terán, of the Zapotec Isthmus of Oaxaca, México, writes of 'The Calling to Write Poetry in an Indigenous Language'. His work, translated by Shook, highlights the danger of disappearing languages, a process set into motion by colonial forced assimilation, dispossession of land and discriminatory laws. Poetry is not only a means of rebellion, but a way of necessity,

> I sing and celebrate the fortune of living; I cry, scream and impotently curse in the face of the injustices of a government that thinks only of business and money; I dream and fight for a better fate for my people and the peoples of the world.

This is realised in poems such as 'Feast of the Dead' where it is presence and joy, rather than grief and absence, that abound. We're given the scene of a Mexican home, replete with marigold flowers, the scent of copal and tables brimming with fruit. It's a poem that pays attention to those who have passed, their voices that persist, that 'slip over' the speakers' 'tongue | like a fish between the hands | of a fisherman'. ('Your Name'). This is precisely the way in which readers move through *Living in Language*. Each essay forms a different plate or element of a dressed table. These are reflections we move through, weighing and sensing their textures and scales, feeling the parts that cling to us, carried over from one musing to the next. I am reminded of a longer autofictional essay that sits at the heart of this compendium. Laura Wittner, in her essay 'Living in Translation', translated by Will Howard, speaks of the gap between selves:

> Does the author feel something from a distance, in her body, while I translate her text? Like a voodoo doll?

As she addresses the available closeness. Here, we find what it means to 'live in language', to make space and gratitude available for our own bodies, and in turn for each other.

> To translate is to inhabit another person. It is to make space inside ourselves, so they, too, may inhabit us.

NOTES ON CONTRIBUTORS

ABDULLAH O. JIMOH is a linguist and a poet. He holds a Bachelor's degree in linguistics and he is a natural language processing enthusiast. His works have appeared or are forthcoming in many journals including *Mudroom, Kalahari Review* and *Afritondo.*

ADAM TAPPER is a student at the University of Chicago Laboratory Schools and an editor of *Ouroboros Review*, the school's translation magazine. He translates German and Yiddish literature and poetry.

ADRIANA LISBOA was born in Rio de Janeiro. With degrees in music and literature, she is the author of many widely translated novels, as well as poetry, short stories, essays, and children's books. Her novel *Crow Blue* was longlisted for the International 2015 IMPAC Dublin Literary Award.

ADRIJA GHOSH is a queer polyglot poet, translator, and writer passionate about diversity and decolonisation in research and the arts. Adrija's debut collection, *the commerce between tongues*, is out with Broken Sleep Books, along with other works in *Gutter Magazine*, *bath magg* and *Wasafiri*.

AILBHE NÍ GHEARBHUIGH has published three collections of poetry in the Irish language and one bilingual collection. She has read at festivals in New York, Paris, Montréal, Berlin and Ballyferriter.

ALEXANDRA BERLINA translates from and into German, Russian, and English. She just finished writing a comedy musical based on *The Master and Margarita* and is looking for a producer.

ALISON ENTREKIN is an award-winning Australian literary translator from the Portuguese. She has translated many of Brazil's most beloved literary works. She won the 2019 NSW Premier's Translation Prize and PEN medallion for her body of work.

ALYA KHAITLINA became known as a poetry prodigy in her early twenties. Born in St Petersburg, she now lives in Germany and works with children.

ASHISH KUMAR SINGH is a queer Indian poet whose work has appeared in *Passages North*, *Chestnut Review*, *The Bombay Literary Magazine*, *Cutleaf Journal*, *The Temz Review*, and elsewhere. Currently, he lives in Lucknow, Uttar Pradesh.

ASWINI KUMAR MISHRA is the author of 12 poetry collections, including two translated into English: *Native Trek* and *Starry Sickle*. He chaired the International seminar on Dalit studies in Lund (2004). He currently lives in Bhubaneswar.

BETH HICKLING-MOORE is a teacher and translator from Portuguese, Spanish and Italian. Her work has appeared in *Circumference*, *The Hooghly Review* and *MPT*, and she is a PELTA emerging translator mentee.

BIBHU PRASAD PADHI has published over 20 volumes of poetry in both English and Odia. He is also a translator and literary critic.

BIDISHA MUKHERJEE is a PhD student in the Department of Humanities and Social Sciences at the Indian Institute of Technology, Kharagpur. She is translating the poetry of Ranajit Das as part of her PhD dissertation.

BILLY RAMSELL's most recent collection, *The Architect's Dream of Winter*, was shortlisted for the 2014 Irish Times Poetry Now Award. It appeared in Italian translation as *Il sogno d'inverno dell'architetto*. He has read his work at many festivals and events around the world.

BOHDAN TOKARSKYI is a literary scholar and translator specialising in Ukraine's twentieth-century and contemporary culture. His essays and translations have appeared in magazines such as *Apofenie*, *Asymptote* and *Los Angeles Review of Books*. He is working on the first English-language monograph on the poetry of Vasyl Stus. He is currently a Research Fellow at the Harvard Ukrainian Research Institute.

BRYNJULF JUNG TJØNN is a critically acclaimed, award-winning Norwegian author. His work explores adoptive identity, belonging, alienation and otherness.

CARLA NYMAN is a poet, playwright and novelist from Palma de Mallorca. She has won the Premio Gloria Fuertes, the accésit Premio Romero Esteo and the Premio Valparaíso de Poesía.

DR CĂTĂLINA FLORINA FLORESCU has a PhD in Comp Lit/Medical Humanities. She is a college educator, mother, person with a hidden disability who has authored 11 books.

CHLOE ELLIOTT is a writer based in York. She is a winner of the 2022 New Poets Prize for her debut pamphlet, *Encyclopaedia*. Her writing features in *bath magg*, *Magma*, *The North* and *Strix* amongst others. She is the current Creative Apprentice for Modern Poetry in Translation.

CSILLA TOLDY is a poet, novelist and translator living in Northern Ireland. She is the recipient of a SIAP award of the Arts Council of Northern Ireland in 2024.

DAVID COLMER is a prize-winning translator of poetry and prose, mainly from Dutch. Recent poetry translations include collections by Radna Fabias, Mustafa Stitou, Nachoem M. Wijnberg and Charlotte Van den Broeck.

DAVID POLLARD got his three degrees from the University of Sussex. He has published eight volumes of poetry. He has translated from Gallego, French and German and other languages.

ESTER NAOMI PERQUIN is a former Poet Laureate of the Netherlands. She has written five poetry collections. An English selection of her work, *The Hunger in Plain View*, was published in 2017.

FIONA SZE-LORRAIN a French writer, musician, poet, literary translator, and editor. Her work includes a novel in stories, *Dear Chrysanthemums* (Scribner, 2023), five poetry collections and over fifteen books of translation.

ILMAR LEHTPERE is an Estonian poet and translator. His translations into English include several prize-winning books of Kristiina Ehin's poems. *Wandering Towards Dawn* (Lapwing, 2010) is a selection of Sadie Murphy's poetry and English versions of his own work.

ISHITA BADURI began writing at a young age and now writes poetry, rhymes, short stories, essays and travelogues. She is known for her acute observation of life, superb artistry, vivid imagery with the absence of any gimmicks.

JENNY HE is a first-year postgraduate researcher in Translation and Transcultural Studies at the University of Warwick. She writes for several literary publications and is a trustee at Charity Translators.

JOSÉ KOZER was born in 1940 in Havana, Cuba, of Jewish parents. He was awarded the Premio de Poesía Iberoamericana Pablo Neruda in 2013. *Tokonoma* was first published in Spain in 2011.

KAREEM JAMES ABU-ZEID PhD is an award-winning translator of poets and novelists from across the Arab world, who translates from Arabic, French, and German.

KINGSHUK SARKAR lives in Kolkata, India and works as a Spanish teacher and translator. His translations of Sambhunath Chattopadhyay's poems have appeared in *Circumference* and other literary journals.

LILIANA DMITROVIC is an artist and a carer who lives in London. She wasn't always from here.

MAMATA NANDA authored the first official Bengali translation of Maya Angelou's collected poems. She has been published in many international anthologies and magazines including *MPT*. Currently she is working on an anthology of contemporary poems by Bengali women.

MARIJA DEJANOVIĆ is a poet and a feminist. She was born in Bosnia and Herzegovina, grew up in Croatia, and currently lives between Croatia and Greece. She has written three poetry collections.

MARTYN CRUCEFIX's recent publications include *Between a Drowning Man* (Salt, 2023) and *Cargo of Limbs* (Hercules Editions, 2019). His translation *Change Your Life, Essential Poems by Rainer Maria Rilke* is published by Pushkin Press in spring 2024.

MINAKSHI PADHI is a well-known name in the world of story writing. She has translated many Odia poets in English.

NAJWAN DARWISH is one of the foremost contemporary Arab poets. His work, hailed as a singular expression of the Palestinian struggle, has been translated into over twenty languages.

NINA MURRAY is an award-winning Ukrainian-American poet and translator. She is the author of the poetry collection *Alcestis in the Underworld* (Circling Rivers Press, 2019) Her translation of Lesia Ukrainka's *Cassandra* was performed at the Omnibus Theatre in London in 2022.

N.S. THOMPSON's translations have appeared in *The Faber Book of 20th Century Italian Poems* (2004) and *Centres of Cataclysm* (Bloodaxe, 2016). His latest chapbooks are *After War* (New Walk, 2020) and *Ghost Hands* (Melos Press, 2020).

OLGA ULTURGASHEVA is a Senior Lecturer in Social Anthropology at the University of Manchester. She is an author and co-editor of three research monographs focusing on environment and human-animal relations.

PRINCESS SHIKISHI (1149–1201) was a Japanese princess and Shinto priestess. She lived her youth in celibacy to devote herself to the gods, and never married. Nonetheless, her poems sometimes speak of the pain of unrequited love. Little is known about her private life, as she left no written words other than her poems.

RABINDRANATH TAGORE was a Bengali polymath. Poet, novelist, and educator; his collection *Gitanjali* won him the Nobel Prize in Literature in 1913. Tagore's work, deeply rooted in spirituality and humanism, continues to influence literature and culture worldwide. He founded Visva-Bharati University and was a key figure in the Bengal Renaissance.

RACHEL RANKIN is a poet, translator and poetry translation researcher based in Edinburgh, Scotland. She translates from the Scandinavian languages, with a particular focus on Norwegian.

RAINER MARIA RILKE was a Bohemian–Austrian poet. He is considered one of the most significant poets in the German language.

RANAJIT DAS is a poet living in Kolkata, India. He has published twelve books of poems, two collections of literary essays and one novel. A collection of his poems in English translation titled *A Summer Nightmare and Other Poems* was published by Rupa & Co. in 2011.

ROBIN MYERS is a poet and translator. Recent translations include *What Comes Back* by Javier Peñalosa M. and *The Brush* by Eliana Hernández-Pachón.

RONYA OTHMANN is an award-winning Kurdish-Yazidi German poet, novelist, essayist and journalist. She received the Orphil debut prize and the Düsseldorf Poetry Debut Award for the poetry collection *intercrime* (2021).

SAIF ANSARI is an Indian writer and freelance illustrator. His work can be found on PoemsIndia as well as on his Instagram page, @hami.asto. Currently, he lives in Bhopal, Madhya Pradesh.

ŞAFAK SARIÇIÇEK, is the son of a Zaza Kurdish-Alevite family, born in Istanbul, presently finishing his legal traineeship at Mosbach Regional Court. Recipient of Baden-Württemberg Art Foundation Grant 2023.

SAMBHUNATH CHATTOPADHYAY (1930–2018) lived in Manirampur, a sleepy town outside Kolkata, India. He worked as a factory worker, hawker, medical representative, deed-writer, guitar teacher, stage performer, and proofreader for a daily newspaper.

SEIJI HAKUI is a Japanese poet living in Tokyo. His debut collection of poems, *Sonnets and Translations*, composed entirely in Classical Japanese, was published in 2022 by Shichosha.

TUOYA WULAN is a writer, translator, and illustrator. She is a graduate student of English literature at Peking University. She hopes to translate vision through words and images.

VASILY KEYMETINOV-BARGACHAN (1941–2020) was an Eveny poet. He published in Eveny, Russian and Sakha. His lyrical voice always echoed the raw beauty of the reindeer herders' land and its enduring spirit.

VASYL STUS (1938–1985) was one of Ukraine's most significant twentieth-century poets, a prose writer, essayist and prolific translator from several languages. As a Ukrainian dissident in the Soviet Union, he spent the last thirteen years of his life in the Gulag, where he wrote his magnum opus collection *Palimpsests* (1980).

VESNA MARIC is an author and translator. She was born in Mostar, Bosnia-Herzegovina and emigrated to the UK in 1992. She is the author of *Bluebird*, a memoir (Granta, UK 2009), and *The President Shop* (Sandorf Passage, US, 2022), a novel, translated into French in 2024. Vesna translates poetry and literary fiction from Croatian to English.

VILMA DE GASPERIN teaches Italian at the University of Oxford. She has published on Italian literature (mainly Vivian Lamarque and Anna Maria Ortese), and the poetry collection *Lezioni di Lingua*.

VIVIAN LEMARQUE was born in Tesero, Italy, in 1946. She has published ten collections of poetry since her first collection *Teresino* (1981) and numerous children's books. She won the Premio Strega (2023) for her latest collection *L'amore da vecchia* (2022).

XINYANG WU is a poet. She is an undergraduate student of Chinese literature and the president of the May Fourth Poetry Club at Peking University. Her poems have appeared in multiple Chinese literary magazines including the 'The Poetry Periodical'.